How Animals Communicate

Series consultant: Michael Chinery

LORENZ BOOKS

This edition is published by Lorenz Books

Lorenz Books is an imprint of Anness Publishing Ltd
Hermes House, 88–89 Blackfriars Road, London SE1 8HA
tel. 020 7401 2077; fax 020 7633 9499
www.lorenzbooks.com; info@anness.com

© Anness Publishing Ltd 2002

This edition distributed in the UK by Aurum Press Ltd, 25 Bedford Avenue, London WC1B 3AT;
tel. 020 7637 3225; fax 020 7580 2469

This edition distributed in the USA and Canada by National Book Network, 4720 Boston Way,
Lanham, MD 20706;
tel. 301 459 3366; fax 301 459 1705;
www.nbnbooks.com

This edition distributed in Australia by Pan Macmillan Australia, Level 18, St Martins Tower,
31 Market St, Sydney, NSW 2000;
tel. 1300 135 113; fax 1300 135 103;
email customer.service@macmillan.com.au

This edition distributed in New Zealand by David Bateman Ltd, 30 Tarndale Grove, Off Bush Road,
Albany, Auckland;
tel. (09) 415 7664; fax (09) 415 8892

A CIP catalogue record for this book is available from the British Library.

Publisher: Joanna Lorenz
Managing Editor: Linda Fraser
Editors: Sarah Uttridge, Rebecca Clunes
Editorial Reader: Richard McGinlay
Production Controller: Claire Rae
Authors: Michael Bright, John Farndon, Dr Jen Green, Tom Jackson, Robin Kerrod, Rhonda Klevansky,
Barbara Taylor
Illustrators: Julian Baker, Peter Bull, Vanessa Card, Stuart Carter, John Francis, Linden Artists,
Rob Sheffield, Sarah Smith, David Webb
Jacket Design: Alix Wood

10 9 8 7 6 5 4 3 2 1

Picture credits
ABPL: 35c /Daryl Balfour: 29bl /Francois Gohier: 44br /Clem Haagner: 31tl /Martin Harvey: 28b,
30tr, 30bl, 31bl, 52bl /Gerald Hinde: 37tl /C Hughes: 18b, 23t /Luke Hunter: 36-37c /Philip Kahl: 28tr
/P Morris: 47br. **E.T Archive:** 16bl. **Adam Britton:** 16tr, 17cl, 19cr, 23br. **Brian and Cherry Alexander:**
33tr, 42br, 43tl. **Ancient Art and Architechture Collection:** /John R Bracegirdle: 21tl. **Ardea London:**
/Liz Bonford:42bl. **Bridgeman Art Library:** 39tr. **BBC NHU:** 40tr /Ingo Arndt: 45bl /Jeff Foott: 33br
/Lockwood and Dattatri: 40tl /Hugh Maynard: 11tlKlaus Nigge: 20tr /Pete Oxford: 7tl /T Pooley 23c
/Anup Shah: 27cr, 51cl /Richard Du Toit: 41b /Tom Walmsley:21c. BBC Wild: 46tl. **M Chinery:** 13cl.
Bruce Coleman: /Peter Evans: 37b /D Green: 12bl /Roine Magnusson: 44tr /Robert Maier: 27t, 26br /
Joe Mcdonald: 32tr, 39br /John Shaw: 38b /Norman Tomalin: 34t, 37tr /Gunter Ziesler: 40b. **Mary Evans:**
13tl. **FLPA:** 56b, 57t /Frank W Lane: 49cr /Philip Perry: 35tr /L S Sorisio: 61bl /Terry Whitaker: 35b. M & P
Fogden: 18t. **Gettyonestone** /24b, 25t /Art Wolf: 43tr. J M Gleeson in The Outing Magazine: 33tl. **Heritage
and Natural History Photography** /Dr John Free: 8a, 7cr, 7bl, 8a. **Kit Houghton:** 24t, 26t. **Innerspace
Visions:** /B Cranston: 60tl, 61br /P Humann: 60bl /D Perrine: 59c /JD Watt: 58tr. **Natural Science Photo
Library:** /M W Powles: 39bl /Lex Hes: 38-39t /David Lawson: 38c /S G Neginhal: 29c /D Allen Photography:
34b. **Nature Photographers Ltd:** 16br. **NHPA:** 27bl, 55t, 55b, 56t, 57b /Mark Bowler: 46br /K Schafer: 17t, 45tl
/Manfred Danegger: 20b /D Heuchlin: 22t /Rich Kirchner: 41c /William Paton: 21b /Christophe Ratier: 51br
/Steve Robinson: 9tl, 51bl, 53tl, 53bl /Andy Rouse: 42t /John Shaw: 33bl. **Oxford Scientific Films:** 54t, 54b,
55cl, 55cr, 57c /Clive Bromhall: 50br,53tl, 53br /Alan and Sandy Carey: 41t /Densey Clyne: 10cl /M Collins: 9cr
/Daniel J Cox: 43b /M P L Fogden: 10tr /M Deeble & V Stone: 19t, 19b /Carol Geake: 27bl /Tim Jackson: 21tr /
Zig Leszczynski: 47cl, 47c /Alistair Macewan: 26bl /Jo Mcdonald: 52tl /Stan Osolinski: 50bl /Andrew Plumptre:
48tl /G Soury: 58bl /Steve Turner: 52tl /Konrad Wothe: 49c /Belina Wright: 47cr /Tom Ulrich: 25br.
Papilio Photographic: 30tr, 35tl. **Planet Earth:** 25b /K&K Ammann: 48b, 49br, 51tr /M Snyderman: 61tl.
Premaphotos Wildlife: 13tr, 13bl, 14bl, 14t, 14br. **Science Photo Library:** 11tr /Dr John Brackenbury: 11cl.
South American Pictures: 59tl. Tony Stone: /Nicholas Parfitt:36b /Manoj Shah: 36t. Roger Tidman: 32b.
Warren Photographic: 10br, 13cr /Jane Burton: 15bl /Kim Taylor: 6tr, 6br, 9bl, 11br, 15tl, 15br, 8br, 8bl.
Front cover main image: **FLPA**

Contents

Communicating in the Wild

Animals 'talk' to each other in many different ways. Most forms of communication are with other individuals of the same kind, but many animals also send signals to other species. These signals are usually concerned with defence. Rattlesnakes, for example, rattle their tails to warn predators or any other large animals that they might get hurt if they get any closer. Many poisonous or bad-tasting insects, including the Monarch butterfly, are brightly coloured. Predators might try them once or twice, but they soon learn that the brightly coloured insects taste bad and should be left alone. Some animals even give out signals to trick their prey. The snapper turtle, for example, attracts fishes to its mouth by waggling its worm-like tongue.

The bright colours of the Monarch butterfly warn predators to stay away.

Communicating with the neighbours

Nearly every species uses some kind of signal to attract mates. Male crickets and grasshoppers attract females with their chirpy 'songs'. Many birds also use songs, although others, including most birds of prey, rely more on spectacular aerial displays. Some male spiders also perform elaborate dances in front of the females. Scents – given out by one or both sexes – play a major role in the courtship and mating of most animals. Mating signals are the only forms of communication used by some solitary animals (those animals that live alone) but most species have a much more complex range of signals.

The most complex 'language' is found among the social animals – those that live in groups and co-operate with each other. They use sounds, visual signals, and scents to pass information to each other. Touching each other is also an important method of giving and receiving information. One of the most amazing forms of communication is the dance language of honeybees. A worker bee finding a good source of nectar returns to the hive and dances on the honey combs. Other workers join in the dance, and the direction and speed of the action tells them the direction and distance of the nectar. They then fly off to collect more of this important food.

Wolves are sociable animals and use touch to bond with each other. They rub bodies, lick each other, and nuzzle each other's fur when they meet.

Communicating by sound

The songs of many male birds attract mates, but they also help to defend a territory by telling other males to keep away. Gibbons and howler monkeys also use sounds to stake out their territories. Chimpanzees are very noisy and excitable animals and they use more than 30 different grunts, screams and hoots to talk to each other. Elephants also make a wide variety of calls, including strange tummy rumbles, some of which can be heard several kilometres away. Dolphins talk to each other by way of an amazing variety of clicks and whistles as they swim through the water.

Dolphins communicate by making high-pitched sound waves by vibrating the air in the passages in their nose. The waves are focused into a beam through the bulge on their head. This sound is then transmitted into the water.

Body language

Many social animals convey their moods and messages by the way they stand or move. Horses and elephants signal to other herd members by moving their ears. The members of a wolf pack all get on well together because each animal knows its place. A low-ranking wolf lowers its head and puts its tail between its legs when it meets a higher ranking individual, as if saying "You're the boss and I won't cause any trouble". A male gorilla makes sure that the other clan members know he is in charge by standing and thumping his chest. Chimpanzees pull faces to indicate their various moods, such as fear, anger, or playfulness. An angry chimp, for example, clenches its lips shut.

Getting close

Chimpanzees, horses, wolves, lions and many other animals spend a lot of time nuzzling and licking each other. This is known as grooming and it helps to keep all the members of a group on good terms. Ants and other social insects also touch and feed each other. This helps to spread the pheromones (bodily scents) that keep the colonies running smoothly.

Gorillas communicate with a variety of sounds, facial expressions and gestures. They stand on their back legs and beat their chests rapidly with their hands. Gorillas very rarely fight with each other, and this is a display to scare away rivals.

When members of a zebra herd meet up, they welcome each other with a series of greeting rituals which include touching and sniffing. Good friends sometimes lay their heads on each other's back.

Bee and Wasp Colonies

Social bee and wasp colonies work like miniature, smooth-running cities. Like good citizens, all the insects in the colony instinctively know their roles and carry out their tasks.

In a honeybee colony, the workers perform different tasks according to their age. The youngest workers stay in the nest and spend their first weeks cleaning out the brood cells. Later they feed the young. As the wax glands in their abdomen develop, they help build new cells. They also keep the nest at the right temperature. After about three weeks, the worker honeybees go outside to fetch nectar and pollen to store or to feed their sisters. The oldest, most-experienced workers act as guards and scouts. Many wasp colonies work in a similar way, with workers doing different jobs according to their age.

▲ **ADJUSTING THE HEAT**
Honeybees are very sensitive to tiny changes in temperature. The worker bees adjust the temperature around the brood cells to keep the air at a constant 34°C. In cold weather, they cluster together to keep the brood cells warm. In hot weather, they spread out to create cooling air channels.

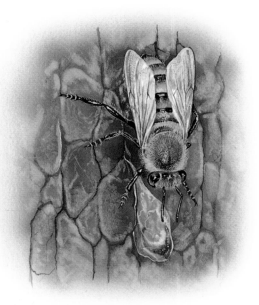

◄ **NEST REPAIRS**
Worker honeybees use a sticky tree resin to repair cracks in their nest. This gummy material is also known as propolis, or 'bee glue'. The bees carry it back to the nest in the pollen baskets on their hind legs. If there is no resin around, the bees may use tar from roads instead.

▲ **BUILDING NEW CELLS**
Honeybee cells are made by workers using wax from their abdomens. The bees use their antennae to check the dimensions of the cells as they must be the right size to fit the young.

◄ **THREAT DISPLAY**

Paper wasp workers from Equador in South America swarm over the outside of their nest to frighten off intruders. Like all wasp workers, one of their main roles is to defend the nest. If this display fails, the wasps will attack and sting their enemy. However, most animals will retreat as quickly as they can.

▲ **PRECIOUS CARGO**

A worker honeybee unloads her cargo of nectar. The bees use the nectar to make honey, which is a high-energy food. The honeybee workers eat the honey, which allows them to survive long, cold winters in temperate regions, when other worker bees and wasps die.

TENDING THE YOUNG ►

A honeybee tends the larvae (young bees) in the nest cells. Honeybees feed their young on nectar and pollen from flowers. Wasp workers feed their larvae on balls of chewed-up insects. The young sister is allowed to feed for about ten seconds, then the worker remoulds the food ball and offers it to another larva. The adult may suck juices from the insect meat before offering it to the young.

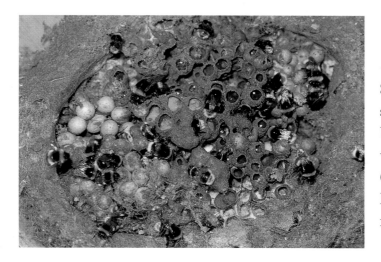

◄ **LITTLE BUMBLEBEE NESTS**

Social bumblebees, shown here, live in much smaller colonies than honeybees. European bumblebee nests usually hold 20–150 insects, whereas a thriving honeybee colony may hold 60–80,000 insects. The queen bumblebee helps her workers with the day-to-day running of the nest as well as laying eggs.

Ant and Termite Societies

Like bee and wasp societies, ant colonies are all-female for much of the year. Males appear only in the breeding season to mate with the young queens. Ant colonies are tended by hundreds or thousands of sterile female workers. The worker ants also fight off enemies when danger threatens, repair and expand the nest, and adjust conditions there. Some ants use the workers from other species as 'slaves' to carry out these chores.

In most types of ants, the large queen is still nimble and active. However, the termite queen develops a huge body and becomes immobile. She relies on her workers to feed and care for her, while she produces masses of eggs.

▲ **ON GUARD**
These ants are guarding the cocoons of queens and workers, who will soon emerge. One of the workers' main tasks is to defend the colony. If you disturb an ants' nest, the workers will rush out with the cocoons of young ants and carry them to a new, safe site.

▼ **RIVER OF ANTS**
Safari ants march through the forest in long lines called columns. The workers, carrying the cocoons of young ants, travel in the middle of the column, where it is safer. They are flanked by a line of soldiers on each side. Resembling a river of tiny bodies, the column may stretch more than 100m.

▲ **ANT RAIDERS**
Slavemaker ants survive by raiding. Here an ant is carrying off a worker from another species. Some slavemakers, such as red Amazon ants, have sharp, pointed jaws that are good for fighting, but no use for other tasks. They rely on ant slaves to gather food and run the nest.

◄ TERMITE SKYSCRAPER

These African termite workers are building a new ventilation chimney for their nest. African termites build the tallest towers of any species, up to 6-7m high. If humans were to build a structure of the same height relative to our body size, we would have to build skyscrapers that were more than 9.5km high. The tallest skyscraper today is less than 500m tall.

FAMILY LIFE ►

A queen termite is flanked by the king (the large insect below her), workers and young termites. The king and queen live much longer than the workers – for 15 years or even more in some species. The queen may lay 30,000 eggs in a day – that is one every few seconds. The king stays at her side in the royal chamber and fertilizes all the eggs.

Did you know? A column of army ants on the march may contain 150,000 insects.

nasute termite
(*Nasutitermes* species)

◄ BLIND GUARD

A soldier termite displays its huge head, which is packed with muscles to move the curved jaws at the front. Being blind, the guard detects danger mainly through scent, taste and touch. Like termite workers, soldiers may be either male or female, but they do not breed. The arch-enemies of these plant-eating insects are meat-eating ants, which hunt them for food.

9

How Social Insects

THE QUEEN'S SCENT
Honeybee workers lick and stroke their queen to pick up her pheromones. If the queen is removed from the nest, her supply of pheromones stops. The workers rear new queens who will produce the vital scents.

Communication is the key to the smooth running of social insect colonies. Colony members interact using smell, taste, touch and sound. Social insects that can see also communicate through sight. Powerful scents called pheromones are the most important means of passing on information. These strong smells, given off by special glands, are used to send a wide range of messages that influence nestmates' behaviour. Workers release an alarm pheromone to rally their comrades to defend the colony. Ground-dwelling ants and termites smear a scent on the ground to mark the trail to food. Queens give off pheromones that tell the workers she is alive and well.

TERMITE PHEROMONES
A queen termite spends her life surrounded by workers who are attracted by her pheromones. The scents she releases cause her workers to fetch food, tend the young and enlarge or clean the nest.

FRIEND OR FOE?
Two black ants meet outside the nest and touch antennae to identify one another. They are checking for the particular scent given off by all colony members. Ants with the correct scent are greeted as nestmates. 'Foreign' ants will probably be attacked.

Communicate

THIS WAY, PLEASE

A honeybee worker exposes a scent gland in her abdomen to release a special scent that rallies her fellow workers. The scent from this gland, called the Nasonov gland, is used to mark sources of water. It is also used like a homing beacon to guide other bees during swarming, when the insects fly in search of a new nest.

ALARM CALL

These honeybees have come to the hive entrance to confront an enemy. When alarmed, honeybees acting as guards give off an alarm pheromone that smells like bananas. The scent tells the other bees to come to the aid of the guards against an enemy. In dangerous 'killer bee' species, the alarm pheromone prompts all hive members to attack, not just those guarding the nest.

SCENT TRAIL

This wood ant worker has captured a worm. The ant is probably strong enough to drag this small, helpless victim back to the nest herself. A worker that comes across larger prey returns to the nest to fetch her comrades, rubbing her abdomen along the ground to leave a scent trail as she does so. Her fellow workers simply follow the smelly trail to find the food. Ants can convey as many as 50 different messages by releasing pheromones and through other body language.

The Butterfly's Mating Quest

common blue butterfly
(Polyommatus icarus)

Butterflies are usually solitary insects. Although hundreds of thousands of them sometimes migrate together, this is not true social behaviour because they do not co-operate with each other. The butterflies don't work together as a group, or communicate. However, all butterflies do need to communicate with each other when looking for a mate.

Most males court females with elaborate flights and dances. Males and females are drawn to each other by the shape of each other's wings and by their colourful patterns. Both sexes also emit pheromones to encourage their mate. Courting butterflies circle each other, performing complicated dances.

▲ COURTING BLUES

When courting a female, a male butterfly often flutters its wings flamboyantly. It looks as if it is showing off, but it is really wafting around its pheromones (the scents from special scales on its forewings). Only if the female picks up these pheromones with her antennae will she be willing to mate.

Did you know? Some butterflies' pheromones are so strong they can be smelt by humans.

◄ THE HAPPY COUPLE

This pair of butterflies is about to mate. When she is ready, the female will fly away and land with her wings half open. The male will flutter down on top of her and begin to caress her abdomen with his rear end. The male then turns around to face the opposite way as they couple. The pair may remain joined like this for hours.

Madame Butterfly

One of the most famous operas is Puccini's Madame Butterfly, written in 1904. The opera is set in the 1800s in Osaka, Japan. It tells the story of an American officer, James Pinkerton, who falls in love with a beautiful young Japanese girl. His nickname for her is Butterfly. They have a child, but Pinkerton abandons Butterfly for his wife in America. The opera ends as Butterfly dies broken-hearted.

▼ SCENT POWER

A butterfly's scent plays a major role in attracting a mate. The scents come from glands on the abdomen of a female. On a male, the scents come from special wing scales called androconia. A male often rubs his wings over the female's antennae.

androconia scales
release scent

▼ COLOURS ATTRACT

Many male butterflies use bright colours to attract mates. This male orange-tip has a distinctive coloured tip to its wings. Females often lack bright colours so are less obvious.

male orange-tip butterfly
(*Anthocharis cardamines*)

▼ SINGLE MATE

Male butterflies mate several times in their lifetime. However a female butterfly usually mates just once and then concentrates on egg-laying. Once they have mated, many females release a special pheromone that deters other males.

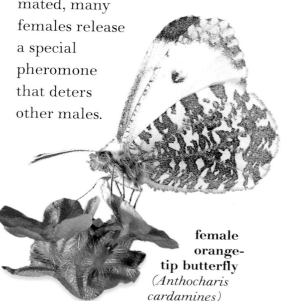

female orange-tip butterfly
(*Anthocharis cardamines*)

▲ FLYING TOGETHER

Butterflies usually stay on the ground or on a plant while coupling. But, if they sense danger, they can fly off linked together, with one (the carrier) pulling the other backwards.

13

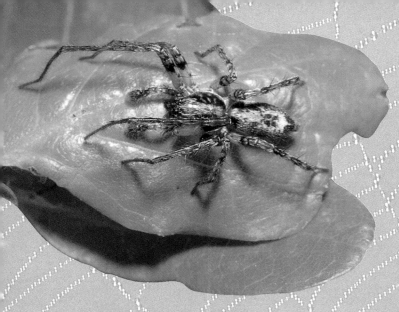

Spider

Although some spiders look after their young, most species only need to communicate with each other when they are ready to mate. Female spiders attract males by giving off pheromones. Each species has a different pheromone, to help the males find the right mate. Once he has found a female, the male has to give out the right signals so that the female realizes he is not a meal. These include special dances, drumming, buzzing, or plucking the female's web in a particular way. Some males distract the females with a gift of food.

NOISY COURTSHIP

The male buzzing spider beats his abdomen against a leaf to attract a mate. The sound is loud enough for people to hear. He often buzzes on the roof of the female's oak-leaf nest. Other male hunting spiders make courtship sounds by rubbing one part of their bodies against another.

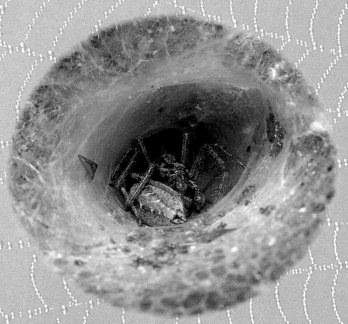

MATING SUCCESS

The male grass funnel-weaver is almost as large as the female and can be quite aggressive. He taps his palps (leg-like feelers) on her funnel web to announce his arrival. If the female is ready to mate, she draws in her legs and collapses as if she is paralysed.

the male presents a gift to the female

BEARING GIFTS

A male nursery-web spider presents an insect gift to the female. He has neatly gift-wrapped his present in a dense covering of very shiny white silk. Once the female has accepted his gift and is feeding, the male can mate with her in safety.

Courtship

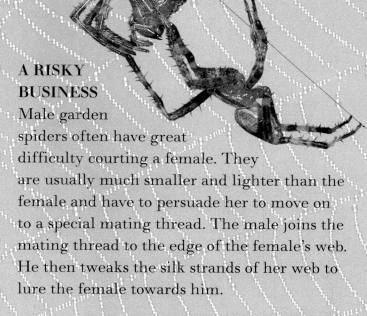

DISTANT DANCE

Spiders that can see well at a distance often dance together before mating. This wolf spider waves his palps like semaphore flags to a female in the distance. Male spiders also strike special poses and use their long, stout front legs to make signalling more effective.

A RISKY BUSINESS

Male garden spiders often have great difficulty courting a female. They are usually much smaller and lighter than the female and have to persuade her to move on to a special mating thread. The male joins the mating thread to the edge of the female's web. He then tweaks the silk strands of her web to lure the female towards him.

DANGEROUS LIAISONS

This male green orb-weaver has lost four of his legs in the process of courting a female. When the female attacked him, he swung down a silken dragline (escape line). He will climb back up again when it is safe.

JUMPING SPIDERS

This pair of jumping spiders are ready to mate. Male jumping spiders impress females by twirling and waltzing, waving their legs, palps and abdomens. Females often attract more than one male and the males have to compete to mate with her. The female reaches out and touches the male when she is ready to mate.

Crocodile Talk

Most reptiles spend very little time with each other, but crocodiles, alligators and other crocodilians have a remarkably sociable life. Groups gather together for basking in the sun, sharing food, courting and nesting.

Crocodilians use sounds, body language, smells and touch to communicate. Adults are particularly sensitive to hatchling and juvenile distress calls and respond with threats or actual attacks. Sounds are made with the vocal cords and with other parts of the body, such as slapping the head against the surface of the water. Crocodilians also use visual communication. Body postures and special movements show which individuals are strong and dominant. Weaker animals signal to show that they recognize a dominant individual and in this way avoid fighting and injury.

▲ **HEAD BANGER**
A crocodile lifts its head out of the water, jaws open. The jaws slam shut just before they smack the surface of the water. This is called the head slap and makes a loud pop followed by a splash. Head slapping may be a sign of dominance and is often used during the breeding season.

The Fox and the Crocodile
In this Aesop's fable, the fox and the crocodile met one day. The crocodile boasted at length about its cunning as a hunter. Then the fox said, "That's all very impressive, but tell me, what am I wearing on my feet?" The crocodile looked down and there, on the fox's feet, was a pair of shoes made from crocodile skin.

▲ **GHARIAL MESSAGES**
The gharial does not head slap, but claps its jaws under water during the breeding season. Sound travels faster through water than air, so sound signals are very useful for aquatic life.

THE LOW SOUND ▶

Some crocodilians make sounds by rapidly squeezing their torso muscles just beneath the surface of the water. The water bubbles up and bounces off the back. The sounds produced are at such a low level we can hardly hear them. At close range, they sound like distant thunder. Very low sounds, called infrasounds, travel quickly over long distances through the water. They may be part of courtship. Sometimes these sounds are produced before bellowing, roaring or head slaps.

Did you know? The bellow of an alligator can be heard at least 150m away.

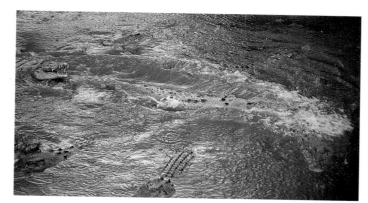

◀ I AM THE GREATEST

Dominant animals are usually bigger and more aggressive than submissive ones. They show off their importance by swimming boldly at the surface or thrashing their tails from side to side on land. When threatened, weaker individuals usually only lift their heads out of the water and expose their vulnerable throats. This shows that they submit and do not want to fight.

GETTING TOGETHER ▶

Caimans gather together at the start of the rainy season in Brazil. Crocodilians often come together in loose groups, for example when basking, nesting or sharing food. The largest, oldest crocodiles dominate the group. Scent glands on a crocodile's jaw and under its tail produce smells that tell the other crocodiles its place in the pecking order. The younger ones steer clear, resting at the fringes of the basking area and avoiding their elders when they are in the water.

Courting Crocodiles

Crocodilians are sociable animals throughout the year, but during the mating season, more communication than usual takes place. Males jostle to become the dominant animal in their stretch of river. They need to establish their social position because the dominant male will mate with most of the females in his territory. Females also need to indicate to their chosen male that they wish to mate.

Courtship behaviour for both male and female crocodilians includes bellowing and grunting, rubbing heads and bodies, blowing bubbles, circling and riding on the partner's back.

▲ POT NOSE

Most male gharials have a strange bump, or pot, on the end of the snout near the nostrils. Females have flat snouts. No-one is quite sure what the pot is for, but it is probably used in courtship. It may help the male to change hissing sounds into buzzing sounds as air vibrates inside the hollow pot.

◄ TOUCHING COUPLE

Crocodilians touch each other a lot during courtship, especially around the head and neck. Males try to impress females by bubbling water from the nostrils and mouth. An interested female arches her back, then raises her head with her mouth open. The two may push each other under the water to see how big and strong their partner is.

◄ SWEET-SMELLING SCENT

Crocodilians have little bumps under their lower jaws. These are called musk glands. The musk is a sweet-smelling, greenish, oily perfume. It produces a scent that attracts the opposite sex. Musk glands are more noticeable in male crocodilians. During courtship, the male may rub his throat across the female's head and neck. This releases the scent from the musk glands and helps to prepare the female for mating.

FIGHTING MALES ►

Male crocodilians may fight each other for the chance to court and mate with females. They may spar with their jaws open or make themselves look bigger and more powerful by puffing up their bodies with air. Saltwater crocodiles are particularly violent and bash their heads together with a loud thud. These contests may go on for an hour or more but do not seem to cause much permanent damage.

◄ THE MATING GAME

A female crocodile often begins the courtship process. She approaches the male and raises her head, exposing her vulnerable throat to show she is no threat. She rubs against the male's head and neck, nudging and pushing him gently. Courtship can last for up to two hours before mating occurs. Both male and female crocodiles court and mate with several different partners.

Feuding Birds of Prey

Birds often squabble over food, and birds of prey (raptors) are no exception. Some birds of prey intimidate others that have already made a kill and try to force them to drop it. This behaviour is called piracy. Sometimes birds of prey are attacked by the birds that they prey on. A number of small birds may join forces against a larger adversary and give chase, usually calling loudly. This is known as mobbing and it generally serves to confuse and irritate the raptor and also warns other prey in the area.

Birds of prey must also defend their nests against predators. The eggs and chicks of ground-nesting raptors are especially vulnerable to attack. Nesting adults will often fly at intruders and try to chase them off.

▲ **SCRAP IN THE SNOW**
On the snowy shores of the Kamchatka Peninsula, in north-east Russia, these sea eagles are fighting over a fish. A Steller's sea eagle, the biggest of all sea eagles, is shown on the right, with its huge wings outstretched. Its opponents, struggling in the snow, are white-tailed eagles. The two kinds of sea eagles are bound to meet and fight, because they occupy a similar habitat and feed on similar prey — fish, birds and small mammals.

◀ **FISH FIGHT**
Two common buzzards fight over a dead fish they have both spotted. Buzzards do not go fishing themselves, but they will feed on any carrion they find.

common buzzards
(*Buteo buteo*)

UNDER THREAT ▶

On the plains of Africa, a dead animal carcass attracts not only vultures, but other scavengers as well. Here, a jackal is trying to get a look-in, but a lappet-faced vulture is warning it off with outstretched wings.

Did you know? Hunters once used eagle owls as bait to attract mobbing birds into range.

jay
(*Garrulus glandarius*)

▲ CLEVER MIMIC

When a jay spots a predator, such as a bird of prey, it gives out an alarm call or mimics the predator's own call to warn other jays.

▲ IN HOT PURSUIT

An osprey has seen this pelican dive into the water and assumes that it now has a fish in its pouch. So it gives chase. Time and again, the osprey will fly straight at the pelican and scare it so much that it will finally release the fish from its pouch.

▼ MOB RULE

A number of crows have ganged up to mob a steppe eagle. They are bold enough to perch dangerously close to their enemy, calling loudly to persuade it to move on. Although the eagle would be more than a match for its tormentors, it might fly off just to escape aggravation.

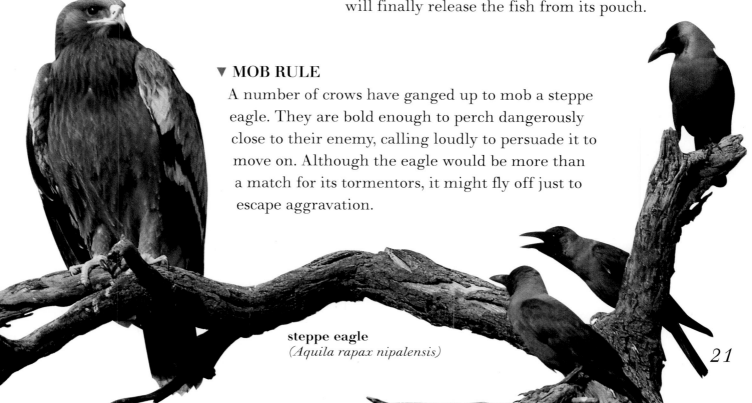

steppe eagle
(*Aquila rapax nipalensis*)

Close Raptor Couples

Most birds of prey stay with their mates for life. However, every year, during the breeding time, the pair strengthen their bonds with each other. This process is called courting.

In courtship displays there is usually a great deal of calling to each other, with the birds close together. The male may offer the female prey that he has caught. This shows her that he is an able hunter and can provide food for her when she is brooding (sitting on eggs) and also provide for their chicks.

Since most birds of prey are superb fliers, however, the most spectacular courtship displays take place in the air. The birds may perform acrobatic dances, or fly side by side, then swoop at each other and even clasp talons. The male may also drop prey whilst in flight for the female to dive and catch in an extravagant game of courtship feeding.

▲ THE MARRIED COUPLE
Like most birds of prey, American bald eagles usually mate for life. They occupy the same nest year after year, gradually adding to it each time they return to breed.

◄ TOGETHERNESS
Secretary birds become inseparable for life once they have paired up, rarely straying apart. Their courtship flights are most impressive, as they fly through the sky with their long tails streaming behind them. They also sleep side by side in their nest throughout the year, not just during the breeding season.

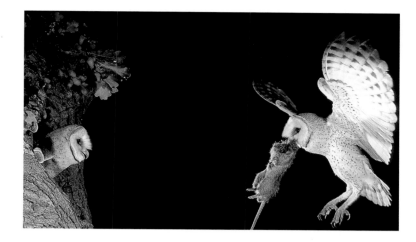

▲ A MOUSE FOR A MATE

A male barn owl has caught a mouse and takes it to his mate back in the nest. This behaviour is called courtship feeding. It helps strengthen the bond between the pair. It is also preparation for the time when the female is nest-bound and incubating their eggs.

▼ BALANCING ACT

A pair of ospreys struggle to keep their balance as they mate on a high perch. The male scrunches up his feet to avoid hurting the female with his talons. Ospreys generally pair for life, but if mating is unsuccessful, they will 'divorce'.

Did you know? Peregrines spend hours performing an amazing courtship flight.

▲ CARACARAS ON DISPLAY

A pair of striated caracaras call to one another by their nest. They are no longer courting but are raising their young. Mated pairs display like this frequently in order to strengthen the bond between them.

▲ FACE TO FACE

A pair of Egyptian vultures stand face to face on the ground as part of an elaborate courtship display. In addition to their ground-based performances, the pair will also perform spectacular aerial displays. They fly, climb and dive close together, often presenting their talons to each other.

osprey
(Pandion haliaetus)

Herds of Horses

Horses, like zebras and asses, are herd animals, and horses living in the wild form what is described as a 'stable' herd. Each member of the herd knows everyone else. The groups are strictly structured, with each animal knowing its place. Stable herds consist of a single stallion with a harem (collection of females and one male) of mares and their foals.

Wild asses and Grevy's zebras have a loose, or 'unstable' herd structure. They live in dry habitats where individual dominant males defend territories that contain water and food. Females live in unstable groups, usually with related animals. They enter the territories of resident males to feed and drink, and so the males will join their herds on a temporary basis.

▲ LEARNING BEHAVIOUR

A foal learns its first lessons on survival from its mother. In a process called imprinting, foals bond to the animal they see most often, which is usually their mother, within a few days of being born. They later learn from watching other members of the herd.

BACHELOR BOYS ▶

These young males have been driven from their herd. At two to three years, they are old enough to form a threat to the reigning stallion. Lone male horses find survival difficult away from the herd. Like these three, they often form small herds called bachelor groups.

◀ **SOCIAL RISE**
Like horses, plains zebras live in a stable herd. Each zebra has its position in the pecking order. Zebras are very sociable animals. They groom one another by nuzzling each other's manes and withers (shoulders) with their front teeth.

▲ **HERD ORDER**
This group of wild horses is a typical herd, consisting of a dominant stallion, six mares and a foal. The foal will have the same social status as its mother until it grows up. It moves up the social ladder as it gains more experience.

FEMALE POWER ▶
Mares and stallions take different roles in the herd. It is usually the dominant mare who decides where to graze and when to move on. The stallion keeps the group together and prevents mares from leaving the herd.

◀ **SEASONAL CHANGE**
Herds do not always remain the same size. These wild asses live in the desert. When food is scarce they live in small groups, but during the wet season they gather in larger groups of up to 50.

Horse Language

Because horses are sociable animals that live in herds, they need to communicate with each other. They have a wide range of expressive behaviour ranging from sounds and smells to a complex body language.

Animals recognize each other by their appearance and smell, and certain sounds are common to all equids. The short whinny is a warning call, while the long version is a sign of contentment. Other calls, such as greetings and aggressive threats, vary from species to species. Horses whinny, asses bray, mountain zebras whistle, and plains zebras bark. Horses, asses and zebras recognize and react to the calls of all other species of equids but do not respond to the calls of cattle or antelope.

▲ **ON YOUR GUARD!**
Horses need to work out where they fit in the social order of the herd. This horse has flattened its ears in a threatening posture — it is showing its dominance. Flattened ears can also indicate boredom or tiredness.

▲ **BABY TALK**
Young horses show respect to their elders by holding their ears to the side, displaying their teeth and making chewing movements. This is not a sign that the foal might bite, but is rather like preparing for a mutual grooming session. It's a way of saying "I'm friendly".

▲ **TAKING NOTE**
Horses are alert to the signals of others. If one horse is curious about something, its ears will prick forwards. The rest of the herd will look to see what has caught its interest.

◀ MUTUAL GROOMING

Horses, like all other equids, will nibble a favourite partner, grooming those places they cannot reach for themselves. The amount of time two horses spend grooming each other shows how friendly they are. Grooming helps to keep a herd together, and it occurs even when the horses' coats are in perfect condition.

FRIENDLY GREETING ▶

When members of a herd meet up, they welcome each other with a series of greeting rituals. They may stretch heads, touch and sniff noses, push each other and then part. Good friends may lay their heads on each other's back.

◀ WILD AT HEART

Mares often develop personal bonds with other horses in the herd. These bonds can form between unrelated mares or with close relatives, such as sisters or adult daughters. The bonds are stronger in all-female herds. In groups led by a stallion, the mares make him their centre of attention. The stallion may have a favourite mare, which he spends a lot of time with.

Elephant Families

An elephant family group is made up of related females and their offspring. Each family is led by an older, dominant female known as the matriarch. She makes all the decisions for the group. Bulls (male elephants) leave their family group when they are between 10 and 16 years old. When they are adults, only the strongest males mate with the females. Bulls spend most of their lives in small, all-male groups or wander on their own. Each family group has close links with up to five other families in the same area. These linked groups make up a herd. An elephant's day follows a regular pattern of feeding, sleeping and travelling to new feeding areas. Meeting, greeting and communicating with other elephants is an important part of every day and interrupts other activities from time to time. Adult elephants co-operate with each other to protect and guide the young.

▲ KEEPING IN TOUCH
A group of elephants drink together. The calves stay close to the group, so that they are continually touched by their mothers, or other close relatives, for reassurance.

▼ FOLLOW MY LEADER
Touch is a vital tool in elephant communication. As the group moves together, they constantly touch each other. In this way, the matriarch controls when they eat, drink and rest. She also protects the group from dangers and controls family members who misbehave.

sire bull
(male parent)

young bulls

juveniles

infants

adult sisters/daughters

matriarch

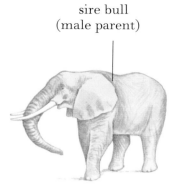

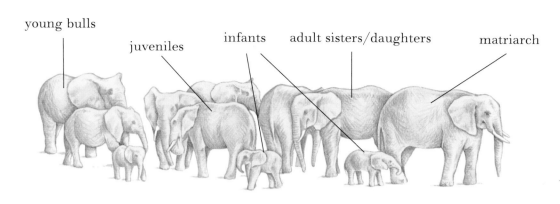

▲ AFRICAN ELEPHANTS

A family of African elephants usually consists of a matriarch, her adult daughters and sisters, their calves and a number of young males and females. Bulls may sometimes join the family for mating but they do not stay with it for long. They soon leave to resume their solitary lives.

◄ SMALL GROUPS

Elephants in Asia live in smaller groups than African elephants. Asian families have between four and eight members, although as many as 10–20 individuals may stay in touch.

◄ ALL ALONE

Male elephants do not form such strong social bonds with each other as the females in family groups do. As a result, some bulls lead entirely solitary lives. However, their calls carry over such a range that it seems likely that, even when out of each other's sight, most bull elephants remain in long-distance communication.

Communicating Elephants

Everyone knows the loud trumpeting sound that elephants make. They make this noise when they are excited, surprised, angry or lost. Elephants also make a wide range of low, rumbling sounds that carry for many kilometres through forests and grasslands. Different rumbles might mean "Where are you?" or "Let's go" or "I want to play". Females can signal when they are ready to mate, and family members can warn each other of danger.

But sound is just one way in which elephants can communicate with one another. They also touch, smell, give off chemical signals and perform visual displays, by altering the positions of the ears and the trunk. Their sense of smell can even tell them about another elephant's health.

▲ ELEPHANT GREETING
When elephants meet, they touch each other with their trunks, smell each other and rumble greeting sounds. Frightened elephants also touch others for reassurance.

BODY LANGUAGE ▶
Elephants send visual signals by moving their ears and trunk. Spreading the ears wide makes the elephant look bigger. This sends a message to a potential attacker to stay away. The elephant also stands up extra tall to increase the threat, raising its tusks, shaking its head and flapping its ears.

Did you know? Humans can only hear about one-third of the sounds an elephant makes.

◄ TRUNK CALL

An elephant makes its familiar high-pitched trumpeting call. Elephants also make a variety of crying, bellowing, screaming, snorting and rumbling sounds. Asian elephants make sounds that African elephants do not, and many of their rumbles last for longer. There are over 20 different kinds of rumble, with females making many more rumbling sounds than males. Females sometimes make rumbling calls when they are together, but male elephants do not do this.

▲ ALARM SIGNALS

This nervous baby elephant is interested in the crocodiles lying on the river bank. It raises its ears, either in alarm or as a threat to the crocodiles. If a baby calls out in distress, its relatives rush to its side, with rumbles of reassurance and comforting touches with their trunks.

▲ TOUCH AND SMELL

An elephant's skin is very sensitive, and touch is an important way of communicating feelings in elephant society. Smells also pass on useful messages, such as when a female or male is ready to mate.

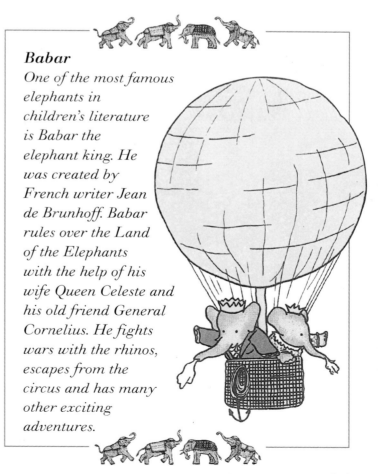

Babar

One of the most famous elephants in children's literature is Babar the elephant king. He was created by French writer Jean de Brunhoff. Babar rules over the Land of the Elephants with the help of his wife Queen Celeste and his old friend General Cornelius. He fights wars with the rhinos, escapes from the circus and has many other exciting adventures.

Bear Aggression

Adult bears are solitary animals. They prefer to wander alone and do not like other bears. When two animals do meet they need to establish which is the dominant one. This sometimes means a fight, but usually it is just a shouting match and display. If one bear can scare away the other without a fight, it means there is less chance of either animal being injured.

Some bears do congregate together in one area at certain times of year, but this is to take advantage of a plentiful food source. Brown bears tolerate each other at fishing rivers and polar bears scavenge together at whale carcasses and rubbish dumps. As soon as the food is gone, the bears resume their solitary life.

▲ STAND TALL

To show aggression, bears rear on their hind legs, as this American black bear is doing. This makes it look bigger and more frightening. The bear will also growl at its opponent and show its teeth.

◄ ICE DANCE

Like two ballet dancers, young male polar bears play at fighting. They use exaggerated lunges and swipes with their paws and jaws. They do not hurt each other, but they must learn to fight well. Later in life as fully grown adults they will compete with other males for females during the breeding season. Fights between well-matched individuals can be violent and often bloody.

The Jungle Book

Rudyard Kipling's famous story The Jungle Book *was first published in 1894. A young boy named Mowgli is brought up by wolves. He is befriended by Baloo the bear and Bagheera the panther who teach him the law of the jungle. The tiger Shere Khan plots to kill the man-cub.*

▲ TRAGEDY ON THE ICE

Adult male polar bears are cannibals. They will kill cubs and feed upon the body. Here a female has attacked and driven away the male, but her cub is unlikely to survive. Male bears are much bigger than females, but a female with cubs is a fierce opponent.

▲ FRIENDS AT THE FEAST

Brown bears gather to catch salmon in Alaska. They use body language, such as ears pointed forward or back, necks stretched or contracted, to avoid conflicts and establish the pecking order.

▲ FISHING BREAK

Young brown bears take a break from learning to fish and practise fighting instead. They fight by pushing and shoving at each other, using their enormous bulk to overcome their opponent. They also try to bite each other around the head and neck.

Big Cat Signals

Although most big cats are solitary, they do communicate with one another. They indicate how old they are, whether they are male or female, what mood they are in and where they live. Cats communicate by signals such as smells, scratches and sounds. The smells come from urine and from scent glands. Cats have scent glands on their heads and chins, between their toes and at the base of their tails. Every time they rub against something, they transfer their special smell. Cats make many different sounds. Scientists know that cats speak to each other, but still do not understand much about their language. Cats also communicate using body language. They use their ears to signal their mood and twitch their tails to show if they are excited or agitated.

▲ A MIGHTY ROAR

The lion's roar is the loudest sound cats make. It is loud enough for all the neighbourhood lions to hear. Lions roar after sunset, following a kill and when they have finished eating. Lions make at least nine different sounds. They also grunt to each other as they move around.

HISSING LEOPARD ▶

An angry leopard hisses at an enemy. Cats hiss and spit when they feel threatened, or when they are fighting an enemy. The position of a cat's ears also signals its intentions. When a cat is about to attack, it flattens its ears back against its neck.

▲ EAR SIGNALS

Many wild cats, such as this tiger, have white markings on the back of their ears. They turn their ears to show the markings to an enemy when they are angry.

▲ CAT SPRAY

A king cheetah marks its territory by spraying urine at points along its trails. Scent marks left by a male tell other males to stay away. The scent left by a female will tell a nearby male if she is ready to mate.

BABY TALK ▶

Mothers talk to their cubs a lot. The sounds are quiet so that enemies do not hear. The softest and safest sound of all is purring.

▲ MARKS FOR SHOW

Cats like to scratch things to clean their claws and stretch their limbs. At the same time they leave a scented mark for others to both see and smell. When this lioness scratches, she leaves her own personal scent from the glands between her toes on the scratch marks.

Did you know? When they are close together, lions chirrup, meow and yowl to each other.

Life in a

Lions live in family groups called prides. A pride may contain 30 or 40 animals consisting of up to 12 lionesses and their cubs and three or four adult males, but many prides may be much smaller. Each pride defends its territory and does not allow other lions to hunt there. Lionesses usually stay in the same pride until they die, but male cubs are driven out when they are about three years old. They roam in small groups called coalitions until they are fully grown. Each coalition attempts to take over an existing pride by killing or driving out the old males.

FATHER AND SON

Male lions are the only big cats that look different from the females. Their long, shaggy manes make them look larger and fiercer and protect their necks in a fight. A male cub starts to grow a mane at about the age of three, he is then driven out of the pride and must establish his own territory.

FAMILY MEETING

A large pride of lions rests near a waterhole. When members of the pride meet, they greet each other with soft moans, swinging their heads from side to side and holding their tails high. Then they head-butt.

Lion *Pride*

NURSERY SCHOOL

Young lions play tag to learn how to chase things and to defend their pride. The pride does not usually allow strange lions to join the family group. Young lions need to be prepared in case other lions come to fight with them.

FIRST AT THE TABLE

Male lions usually eat first, even though the females do most of the hunting. Lions are the only cats that share their feast. All other cats kill prey and eat alone.

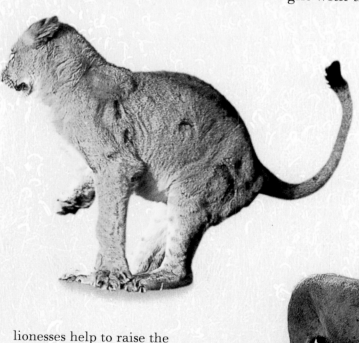

CAT SCRAP

Two lionesses fight each other to decide who will be the first to eat. There is usually a dominant female in each pride, even when there are males around. This chief female rules the family.

MOTHER AND CUBS

Lionesses give birth to a litter of between one and six cubs. Male cubs stay with their mother for over two years and the females usually stay for a lifetime. The mother calls her cubs to her with a soft growl and they respond.

lionesses help to raise the young together and even suckle each other's cubs

Cat Communication

The social lions are the exception among big cats. Most cats lead solitary lives. They hunt alone and the females bring up their cubs alone. Big cats come together only when they want to mate. Their loner lifestyle has evolved because of their need to find food. There is usually not enough prey in one area for a large group of big cats to live on.

All wild cats have territories which they defend from other cats. These areas will include a hunting area, drinking places, lookout positions and (for females) a den where she brings up her young. Female cats have smaller territories than males. Males that have more than one mate have territories that overlap with two or more female territories.

Did you know? Big cats' territories range from a few kilometres to over 1,000km.

▲ BRINGING UP BABY

Female snow leopards bring up their cubs on their own. They have up to five cubs who stay with their mother for at least a year. Although snow leopards are loners, they are not unsociable. They like to live near each other and let other snow leopards cross their territories.

◄ THE LOOKOUT

A puma keeps watch over its territory from a hill. Pumas are solitary and deliberately avoid each other except during courtship and mating. The first male puma to arrive in an area claims it as his territory. He chases out any other male that tries to live there.

Daniel and the Lions' Den
*A story in the Bible tells how Daniel was
taken prisoner by Nebuchadnezzar, king of
Babylon. When Daniel correctly interpreted
the king's dreams he became the king's
favourite. His enemies became jealous of his
position and had him thrown into a lions'
den, a common punishment for
prisoners at the time. But instead
of eating Daniel, the lions
befriended him. They
were
tamed
by his
great faith
in God.*

▲ A PRIDE OF LIONS

The lions in a pride drink together, hunt
together, eat together and play together. They
try to avoid contact with other prides. To tell
the others to keep out of its territory, the pride
leaves scent markings on the edge of its range.

▲ FAMILY GROUPS

A cheetah mother sits between her two cubs.
The cubs will leave their mother at about 18
months old and the female then lives alone.
Males, however, live in small groups and
defend a territory. Male cheetahs are the only
big cats apart from lions to live in groups.

▲ WELL GROOMED

Cats that live together groom each other. They
do this to be friendly and to keep clean. Cats
also groom to spread their scent on each other,
so that they smell the same. This helps them
to recognize each other and identify strangers.

The Communities of Wolves

Wolves are very social animals. A few may live alone, but most live in packs. Most wolf packs have between 8 and 24 members. The main purpose of living in a pack is to hunt. A team of wolves working together can hunt down and kill much larger and stronger prey than a solitary wolf could. Only the strongest, healthiest pair in the wolf pack will actually mate. Every pack member then helps to feed and bring up the cubs.

Other canids have a similar social structure. Bush dogs, dholes and African hunting dogs also live in packs, while jackals, and sometimes coyotes and raccoon dogs, live in smaller family groups. Maned wolves and foxes usually live alone and prey on smaller animals.

▲ TWO'S COMPANY
A pair of jackals drink from a water hole in South Africa. Most jackals pair up for life and co-operate over rearing their pups. Jackals also work together when hunting. They use yips, growls, hisses and howls to work together to hunt down their prey.

Did you know? Foxes produce alarming screams when looking for a mate.

ON PATROL ▶
A wolf pack is led by the strongest, most experienced animals. Every morning the pack patrols the edges of its territory, making fresh scent markings and checking for strange scents that will tell them if rival wolves have been there.

maned wolf
(*Chrysocyon brachyurus*)

▲ A FAMILY AFFAIR

Dholes live in family packs of between five and twelve animals. Sometimes several families join together to form a large dhole pack called a clan. Hunting in a big group helps these relatively small wild dogs to tackle large prey such as wild cattle and buffalo.

▲ EACH FOR ITSELF

The maned wolf is mostly solitary, living and hunting rodents on its own. It does not howl, but barks, whines and yaps like a domestic dog. It also growls when it is frightened or preparing to attack.

◄ COYOTE COUPLE

Most coyotes live and hunt alone, in pairs or in small family units. Coyotes mark their territory with urine or faeces. The smell warns intruders that another coyote is living here and to stay away.

DOG SOCIETY ►

African hunting dogs are the next most social canids after wolves, and hunt co-operatively. Unlike most other canids, however, African hunting dogs are not territorial and do not make scent markings with their urine.

Living in

A wolf pack has a strict social order and each member knows its place. The senior male and female, known as the alpha male and female, are the only animals to breed. The alpha male takes the lead in hunting, defends the pack members from enemies, and keeps the other animals in their place. In most packs, a second pair of wolves, called the beta male and female, come next in the ranking order. The other pack members are usually the offspring of the alpha pair, aged up to three years old.

LEADER OF THE PACK

An alpha male wolf greets a junior pack member. Wolves use different body positions and facial expressions to show rank. The leader stands upright with tail held high. The junior has his ears laid back and his tail tucked between his legs.

IT'S A PUSHOVER

A junior wolf rolls over on its back in a gesture of submission to a more dominant pack member. A junior wolf can also pacify a stronger animal by imitating cub behaviour, such as begging for food.

SHOWING WHO IS BOSS

A wolf crouches down to an alpha male. The young wolf whines as it cowers, as if to say, "You're the boss." The pack leader's confident stance makes him look as large as possible.

a Wolf Pack

"I GIVE UP"

A male grey wolf lays its ears back and sticks its tongue out. Taken together, these two gestures signal submission. A wolf with its tongue out, but its ears pricked, is sending a different message, showing it feels hostile and rebellious.

REJECTED BY THE PACK

Old, wounded or sickly wolves are often turned out of the pack to become lone wolves. Although pack members may be affectionate with each other, there is no room for sentiment. Young wolves may also leave to start their own packs. Lone wolves without the protection of a pack are much more vulnerable to attack and must be more cautious.

SCARY SNARL

A grey wolf bares its canine teeth in a snarl of aggression. Studies have shown that wolves use up to 20 different facial expressions. Junior wolves use snarling expressions to challenge the authority of their leaders. The alpha male may respond with an even more ferocious snarl. If it does so, the junior wolf is faced with a choice. It must back down, or risk being punished with a nip.

Primates Living Together

All primates communicate in some way with other members of their species, and most of them live in social groups. Community living has advantages. There are more eyes to spot predators, and several animals can work as a team to fight off attack or forage for food. As a community, they stand a better chance of survival if there is a problem with the food supply, during a drought, for instance. The leaders will feed themselves and their young first to make sure that they survive. Solitary animals may have a hard time finding a mate, but within a group, there's plenty of choice. And, when there are young to be cared for, a community can provide many willing helpers.

Nocturnal prosimians rely on being solitary and silent to avoid being noticed by predators. Among bush babies and lorises, even couples live independently of each other, but they occupy the same patch, and their paths often cross. Babies stay with their mother until they are old enough to live alone.

▲ TREE-SHARING
Sifakas work together in groups of about seven adults to defend their territory. They are generally led by the females, and males may swap between groups. These prosimians gather in the higher branches of the trees in western Madagascar. If danger threatens, they all start a hiccuping groan.

HAPPY COUPLE ▶
In the jungles of South America, male and female sakis mate and usually live as a couple for a year. The female cares for the young. The father may not spend the day with his family, but does return to them at night. If there is plenty of food, families mingle with each other, forming large, loosely-knit groups.

44

◄ FEMALE RULE

A female is in charge of this troop of black tufted-ear marmosets. As with most other New World marmosets and tamarins, there may be several other females, but only the head female breeds. She mates with all the males to make sure her top-level genes are passed on. As none of the males knows who is the father, they all help rear and protect the young.

EQUAL SOCIETY ►

The relationship between a woolly monkey mother and her children can last for life. Woolly monkeys live in troops — there may be 20 to 50 of them, with roughly equal numbers of males and females. Adult males often cooperate, and all the males and females can mate with each other. Individual females care for their own young. Woolly monkey groups are bound by an intricate web of relationships between all members that is hard for outsiders to understand.

◄ MALE POWER

These female hamadryas baboons are just two in a harem of several females. A single, top male mates with all the females to make sure he fathers all the children. Males with no harem live in separate bachelor groups of two or three. They try to mate with a harem when the leader is not looking. When the leader gets old, a few young males will team up to depose him. Once he has been chased away, the victors fight for control of the harem.

45

Monkey Signals

Attracting attention in a noisy forest is a challenge. Groups of tree-living monkeys and prosimians lose sight of each other and keep in touch by calling. Nocturnal prosimians, however, need to keep a low profile, and so they leave scent messages that are easier to place accurately.

All prosimians and, to a lesser extent, monkeys, send messages of ownership, aggression or sexual readiness with strong-smelling urine, or scent from special glands. Monkeys can also express their feelings with facial expressions and gestures, and some use their ability to see in colour. African guenons, for example, have brightly coloured patches on their bodies that can be seen by their companions when they are hurtling through the trees. Even fur and tails can be useful. Ring-tailed lemurs swish their tails menacingly at rivals, and at the same time, fan evil smells over them.

▲ DON'T HURT ME

This toque macaque is showing by its posture and expression that it is no threat. If an adult monkey wants to make friends, it may make a sound like a human baby gurgling. The other monkey will usually respond gently.

Did you know? Monkeys have more face muscles than prosimians and pull more expressions.

PERSONAL PERFUME ▶

A black spider monkey smears a strong-smelling liquid on a branch. The liquid is produced by a gland on the monkey's chest. Its smell is unique to this monkey. When other monkeys smell it, they know that another of their kind has been there. If they meet the particular monkey that left the scent, they will recognize it.

◀ TELL-TAIL SIGNS

In complicated langur societies, high-ranking males hold their tails higher than lesser members of the group. Primates that live in complex social groups have a wider range of communication skills than solitary species. More information has to be passed around among a greater number of individuals.

▲ YOU SCRATCH MY BACK . . .

Grooming a fellow monkey not only gets rid of irritating fleas and ticks, but also forges a relationship. A lot of monkey communication is about preventing conflicts among group members. Forming strong personal bonds hold the troop together.

▲ BE CAREFUL

A mandrill has mobile face muscles to make different expressions. Here, he pulls back his gums and snarls. This makes him look very menacing to other males.

▲ I'M ANGRY

When a mandrill becomes angry, he opens his mouth in a wide yawn to show the size of his teeth and roars. Another monkey will hesitate before confronting this male.

LOOKING FIERCE ▶

This marmoset is literally bristling for a fight. Its fur stands on end like an angry cat's to make it look much bigger. It may scare its rival into withdrawing. Marmosets look cute, but they squabble a lot among themselves.

Ape Groups

Of all the apes, chimpanzees live in the largest groups – up to about 100 individuals. The chimps constantly change their friends and often drop out altogether to spend time on their own. A chimpanzee group is based around the most important male chimps. Gorilla groups are similar but smaller, led by a strong adult male called a silverback. Bonobos live in smaller groups than chimpanzees, but their society is led by females rather than males. Orangutans tend to live on their own, although females and their young spend a lot of time together while the youngster is growing up. Gibbons have a completely different social system from that of other apes – they live in family groups of a mother, father and their young.

▲ GENTLE GIANTS

Life in a gorilla group is generally friendly and there is seldom serious fighting within the group. The silverback (named for the white hair on its back) can stop most squabbles by strutting and glaring at the troublemakers. He is the group's leader, deciding where it will travel and where it will settle.

Did you know? Bonobos can understand language as well as a human toddler.

bonobos
(*Pan paniscus*)

▼ SOCIABLE SOCIETY

Bonobos are very sociable creatures. Most of the time they live in large, loose groups, called communities, which are split up into smaller groups of 15 or less when foraging for food.

juvenile male

male silverback leader

adult female

young gorilla

◀ HAPPY FAMILIES

Gorillas like to live in extended family groups, usually with between five and thirty members. A gorilla without a group will do its best to join one or start a new one. Each group is controlled and defended by a silverback.

▲ TREETOP SINGERS

Gibbons live in family groups and are the only apes to mate for life. A mated pair of gibbons 'sing' a loud duet to declare their territory to other gibbons in the forest. The male hoots, whoops and wails, while the female makes a rising twitter.

LONE ORANG ▶

Orangutans spend most of their time alone. One reason for this may be that they need to eat a lot of fruit every day. If lots of orangutans lived together, they would not be able to find enough fruit to eat. Even when they do meet, they often ignore each other.

BEST FRIENDS ▶

Females form the backbone of a bonobo group. Adult female bonobos form strong friendships, which are reinforced by grooming and hugging each other. This group of female bonobos have been raised in captivity. Boredom in captivity leads some apes to pluck out their hair.

bonobos
(Pan paniscus)

Great Ape Language

▼ GIBBON DUET
As well as warning other gibbons to stay out of their territories, the duet sung by gibbon pairs may also help to strengthen the bond between them. The pair will also use facial expressions to show feelings such as fear and excitement.

Although apes cannot speak, they communicate with a variety of sounds, facial expressions and gestures. Scientists have even learned some of this ape-speak in order to reassure the apes they are studying, and avoid frightening the animals away. Orangutans and gibbons both call loudly to stake their claim to their territory, rather as we would put up a fence and a 'keep out' sign around our property. In chimp and gorilla societies, body positions and gestures show which animals are most important, or dominant, and which are least important, or submissive. Chimps and gorillas also communicate through a variety of sounds, especially chimps, who can be very noisy apes.

▲ PULLING FACES
Chimpanzees have a variety of different expressions for communication. A wide, open and relaxed mouth is a play face used to start, or during, a game. An angry chimp clenches its lips shut.

siamang gibbon
(Hylobates syndactylus)

◄ A GAME OF BLUFF

Rising on his back legs, a male silverback gorilla slaps his cupped hands rapidly against his chest, making a 'pok-pok-pok' sound. Then he charges forwards, tearing up plants and slapping the ground. This display is really a bluff to scare away rivals. Gorillas hardly ever fight, and a male usually stops his charge at the last minute.

▲ GORILLA-SPEAK

Researchers observing gorillas in the wild have learned to make the same sounds and gestures as the gorillas. A content gorilla makes a rumbling belch sound. A sharp, pig-grunt noise means the gorilla is annoyed.

◄ KEEP OUT!

Fully grown male orangutans usually keep to a particular area of forest – up to 10 sq km. This is called their home range. Every day, a male roars loudly to warn other orangutans to stay away. This long call lasts for about two minutes. By calling, males avoid meetings that might end in a fight.

TOP CHIMP ►

The dominant chimpanzee in a group shows off occasionally by charging about, screaming and throwing branches. He also hunches his shoulders and makes his hair stand up on end.

▼ LOW RANK

To avoid fighting with important chimps, low-ranking chimps behave in a certain way. They flatten their hair, crouch down or bob up and down, and back towards the more important chimp, while pant-grunting.

The Close

All the chimpanzees in a community know each other well. Mothers have a very strong bond with their young, and many chimps who are not related form close friendships, especially males. Dominant males form the stable core of a chimpanzee group and they will attack and even kill males from other communities. Female chimps may emigrate to a neighbouring community. Members of a community will meet, spend time together and then separate throughout the day. In chimp society there is a hierarchy of importance, which is maintained by powerful males. The chimps jostle for position, constantly checking where they stand with each other and challenging their leaders.

YOU GROOM MY BACK

One of the most important activities in a chimpanzee group is grooming. It helps to keep the group together by allowing the chimps to strengthen friendships and patch up quarrels. High-ranking chimps are often groomed by low-ranking ones. It takes a young chimp about two years to learn how to groom properly.

MOTHERS AND BABIES

For the first three months of its life, a baby chimpanzee clings to its mother. By watching her face, it learns to copy her expressions of fear, anger and friendship. The bond between a mother chimpanzee and her young is very strong, and lasts for many years. In fact, the closest relationships within the family group are between a mother and her grown-up daughters.

Chimp Group

GANG WARFARE

A dominant male chimp often makes friends with two or three others, who spend time with him and back him up in fights. Powerful supporters enable a chimp to become a leader.

PLAYTIME

As young chimpanzees play, they get to know how to mix with the other chimps in a group. They learn how to greet others and which individuals are the most important.

FRIENDSHIP

To show their affection for one another, chimps hug, kiss and pat each other on the back. As males spend much more time together than females, this friendly contact is more common between males, although females strike up special friendships, too.

NOISY CHIMPS

Chimpanzees make more than 30 different sounds. When they are contented, they make soft 'hooing' noises, when they discover food they hoot, and when they are excited they scream.

Whale Life

Many toothed whales — which eat fish and squid — are sociable and live together. Sperm whales live in groups of up to about 50. A group may be a breeding school of females and young or a bachelor school of young males. Older male sperm whales usually live alone. Beluga whales often live in groups of several hundred.

Baleen whales are not as sociable and move singly or in small groups. This is probably because they filter huge amounts of small creatures out of the water as they swim — they could not find enough food if they lived close together.

Did you know? Dolphins will nudge a sick member of the group up to the surface, so it does not drown.

▲ **HERD INSTINCT**
Beluga whales gather together in very large groups, or herds. They are noisy creatures whose voices can clearly be heard above the surface. This is why they are sometimes called sea canaries. Belugas have a wide range of facial expressions and often appear to be smiling.

▼ **BONDED ORCAS**
Two killer whales, or orcas, rise out of Antarctic waters together, as if on a signal. They are members of the same pod, or group, which stay together all their lives. The bonds between the animals are very strong. This helps them co-ordinate their activities, especially when they are hunting for food.

Did you know? Male whales often try to help injured females. Females rarely try to help injured males.

◄ STAYING CLOSE

Two Atlantic spotted dolphins swim with their young. Mother and young often play together, turning, rolling, and touching each other with their flippers. During play, the young dolphins learn the skills they need in later life.

▼ HUMAN CONTACT

A bottlenose dolphin swims alongside a boy. These dolphins usually live in social groups but lone animals often approach humans.

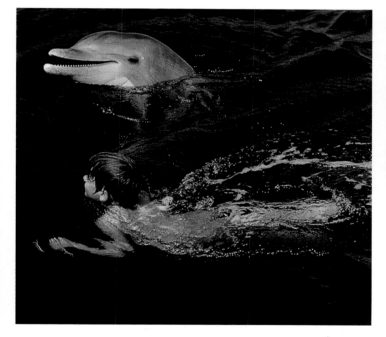

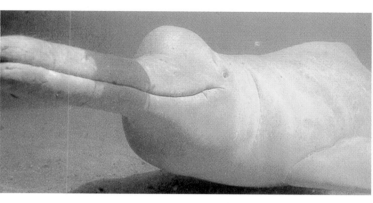

▲ SOLITARY SWIMMER

An Amazon river dolphin rests on the river bed. It spends most of its life alone, or with just one other. This solitary behaviour is typical of river dolphins, but untypical of most ocean dolphins and whales.

HELP AT HAND ►

These long-finned pilot whales are stranded on a beach. Pilot whales usually live in large groups, with strong bonds between group members. One whale may strand itself on a beach. If others try to help they may also get stranded.

Dolphins at Play

Dolphins delight people with their acrobatic antics. They somersault, ride the bow waves of boats and go surfing. Dusky and spinner dolphins are particularly lively. In most animal species only the young play. In whale and dolphin society, adults play too. Often the animals seem to perform just for fun. But some antics have a purpose, such as sending signals to other dolphins.

Dolphins also use whistles and clicking sounds to communicate. Each dolphin has a signature 'whistle' to identify it. As each dolphin 'talks' the other one listens.

▲ PLAYFUL PAIR
Two Atlantic spotted dolphins jostle as they play with a sea fan. Dolphins spend much of their time playing, especially the younger ones. They make up games, using anything they can find. Their games can last for many hours.

▼ JUMPING FOR JOY
A pair of bottlenose dolphins leap high, leaving the water together, as if they have rehearsed their act. They seem to jump for joy, but their behaviour may have a social function within their family group.

► PORPOISING ON PURPOSE

A group of long-snouted spinner dolphins go porpoising, this is where they take long, low leaps as they swim. They churn the water behind them into a foam. Many dolphins practise porpoising, in order to travel fast on the surface.

Did you know? Killer whales like brushing against each other as they swim at high speed.

◄ RIDING THE WAKE

A Pacific white-sided dolphin surfs the waves. This is one of the most acrobatic of the dolphins, like other species of dolphins it likes to ride in the waves left in the wake of passing boats.

Did you know? The rough skin on a porpoise's back may be for giving calves piggy-back rides.

AQUATIC ACROBAT ►

This dusky dolphin is throwing itself high into the air. It twists and turns, spins and performs somersaults. This behaviour is like a roll call — to check that every dolphin in the group is present and ready to go hunting. The behaviour is repeated after hunting to gather the group together once more.

Did you know? A dolphin may play cat and mouse with its prey before eating it.

The Sharks' Pecking Order

No shark is alone for very long. Sooner or later, one shark will come across another, including those of its own kind. In order to reduce the risk of fights and injury, sharks talk to each other, not with sound, but with body language. Sharks have a clear pecking order. The bigger the shark, the more important it is. Not surprisingly, small sharks tend to keep out of the way of larger ones. Many species use a sign that tells others to keep their distance. They arch their back, point their pectoral fins down and swim stiffly. If this doesn't work, the offending shark will be put in its place with a swift bite to the sides or head. Bite marks along its gill slits can be a sign that a shark has stepped out of line and been told firmly to watch out.

▲ A COUPLE OF CHUMS
Great white sharks were once thought to travel alone, but it is now known that some journey in pairs or small groups. Some sharks that have been identified by scientists will appear repeatedly at favourite sites, such as California's Farallon Islands, 42km off the coast of San Francisco. There they lie in wait for seals.

Did you know? Male sharks bite females to encourage them to mate.

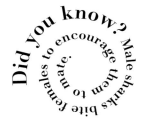

◄ BED FELLOWS
Sharks, such as these whitetip reef sharks, will snooze alongside each other on the seabed. They search for a safe place to rest below overhanging rocks and coral, where, as fights rarely break out, they seem to tolerate each other. The sharks remain here until dusk, when they separate to hunt.

◄ ATTACK MARKS
This grey reef shark has swum too close to another, larger shark and has been bitten on its gill slits as a punishment. The marks on its skin show that its attacker raked the teeth of its lower jaw across the sensitive skin of the grey reef's gill slits. A shark's injuries heal rapidly, so this unfortunate victim will recover quickly from its wounds.

REEF SHARK GANGS ►
Sharks have their own personal space. When patrolling the edge of a reef, the blacktip reef sharks will tell others that they are too close by moving their jaw or opening their mouth. During feeding, order sometimes breaks down and a shark might be injured in the frenzy.

◄ SHARK SCHOOL
Every day schools of scalloped hammerhead sharks gather close to underwater mountains in the Pacific Ocean. They do not feed, even though they come across shoals of fish that would normally be food. Instead, they swim repeatedly up and down, as though taking a rest.

59

Schools for

BAD-TEMPERED SHARKS

The larger a female hammerhead becomes, the less likely she is to get on with her neighbours. Older and larger hammerhead sharks like more space than smaller, younger sharks. In hammerhead schools, the relationship between sharks seems to be controlled by constant displays of threat and small fights.

FEMALES ONLY

The sharks in this huge school of hammerheads are mainly females. The larger sharks swim in the centre and dominate the group, often butting one another to choose the best positions in which to swim. Not only is the middle safer, but it is also the place where the male sharks will be on the lookout for a mate.

By day scalloped hammerhead sharks swim in large groups called schools around underwater volcanoes in the Pacific, off the coast of Mexico, and the Cocos and Galapagos islands. This species of shark cannot stop swimming or it will drown, so schools are a safe resting place for them. Even sharks have enemies, such as other sharks and killer whales, and there is safety in numbers. In schools, scalloped hammerheads can also find a mate. At night, they separate to hunt. They swim to favourite feeding sites, they are thought to use their electric sensors to find their way.

Hammerheads

CLEAN UP OPERATION

At some gathering sites, such as Cocos Island in the eastern Pacific, sharks drop out of the school and swoop down to cleaning stations close to the reef. From the reef, butterfly fish dart out to eat the dead skin and irritating parasites that cling to the outside of the shark's body.

BODY LANGUAGE

Larger sharks within a school perform strange movements and dances to keep smaller sharks in their place. At the end of the movement, a large shark may nip a smaller one on the back of the head.

STRANGE HEAD

The scalloped hammerhead is so named because of the grooves along the front of its head, which gives it a scalloped (scooped out) appearance. The black tips on the underside of its pectoral fins are another way of identifying this shark.

Glossary

abdomen
The middle section of an animal's body. It holds the reproductive organs and part of the animal's digestive system.

alarm
Sudden fear that is produced by an awareness of danger.

antennae
A pair of long jointed structures on the head of invertebrates (especially insects) which act as feelers.

body language
The communication of information by means of conscious or sometimes unconscious bodily gestures and facial expressions.

bonding
The forming of strong emotional attachments, especially between a mother and her baby.

bray
A loud cry that asses and zebras make, sounding like a loud laugh.

canid
A member of the dog family, which includes wolves, jackals, coyotes and foxes.

carcass
The dead body of an animal.

carnivore
An animal that feeds on the flesh of other animals.

carrion
The remains of a dead animal.

colony
A group of the same species of animal or plant that live close together.

conflict
A disagreement or fight between two or more animals.

congregate
To gather in a crowd.

courtship
To woo or court an intended mating partner.

crocodilian
A member of the group of animals that includes crocodiles, alligators, gharials and caimans.

dominance
A system between animals, such as lions, in which one or a few animals rule the group and have first choice over the other, more junior members.

equid
Any Horse or horse-like animals, such as asses and Zebras.

groom
The way an animal cares for its coat and skin. It can be carried out by the animal itself or by one animal for another.

habitat
The particular place where an animal lives.

harem
A collection of female animals overseen by a single male.

herd
A group of particular animals that remain together, such as elephants or wildebeest.

infrasounds
Very low frequency sounds. These are produced by crocodiles by bellowing, roaring or head slaps.

insect
An invertebrate (lacking a backbone) animal that has three body parts, six legs and usually two pairs of wings. Ants, bees and butterflies are all insects.

invertebrate
An animal that does not have a backbone, such as an insect.

Latin name
The scientific name for a species. An animal often has many different common names. For example, the bird called an osprey in Europe is often referred to as a fish hawk in North America. The Latin name prevents confusion because it does not alter.

matriarch
The female head of a group, e.g a queen bee.

migrate
When animals, especially birds, travel from one region to another at certain times of year. Many birds fly to warmer climates for the winter months.

mobbing
When prey birds gang up against their predators and try to drive them away.

pack
A collection of animals that live and feed together in a group, e.g dogs and wolves.

palps
Short stalks that project from the mouthparts of a butterfly, moth or spider which act as sense detectors. They play an important part in finding food and food plants.

pecking order
A social hierarchy that exists among some animal groups.

pheromone
A chemical scent released by animals to attract members of the opposite sex.

piracy
When a bird of prey is intimidated by another into dropping the kill that it has made.

posture
The way that an animal holds its body whilst standing, sitting or walking. Posture can show others that it is strong and dominant.

predator
An animal that catches and kills other animals for food.

prey
An animal that is hunted by other animals for food.

pride
A group of lions.

primate
A group of mammals that includes monkeys, apes and humans. They all have flexible fingers and toes and forward facing eyes.

prosimian
The group of primates that includes lemurs, lorises, pottos and tarsiers. Prosimians have smaller brains than other primates.

reptile
A scaly, cold-blooded animal with a backbone, including tortoises, turtles, snakes, lizards and crocodilians.

ritual
A procedure or actions that are repeated regularly.

scavenger
An animal that feeds on the remains of dead animals.

scent
A smell. For instance, social insects give off scents to give a wide range of messages that influence the behaviour within the nest.

signal
A message in the form of sound or a gesture. A wolf's howl will gather a pack together for a hunt.

sociable animal
An animal that prefers to be in the company of other animals rather than being alone, e.g. lions.

social animal
An animal that lives in a group with other animals of its own kind, e.g. horses and elephants. They co-operate with other group members.

solitary
Animals that prefer to live alone and without companions, e.g. snakes.

species
A group of animals that share similar characteristics and can breed together.

stable herd
A group of equids, including horses and plains zebras, that form a permanent herd. Their bonds are to each other and not a particular territory.

talon
A hooked claw, especially on a bird of prey.

termite
An ant-like social insect that lives in highly organized colonies, mainly in tropical areas.

territory
An area that an animal uses for feeding or breeding. Animals defend their territories against others of the same species.

vertebrate
Any animal with a backbone, including reptiles, birds and mammals.

whinny
The gentle neighing noise made by a horse.

Index

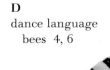